BAMBOO BLADE
10
D0665518
Mid-Continent Public Library
15616 East US Highway 24
Independence, MO 64050

BAMBOO BLADE 10
CONTENTS

Chapter ⑦⑨:
The Muroe High Kendo Team and Burnish Academy..... 3
Chapter ⑧⓪:
TV and Commercials 29
Chapter ⑧①:
Teramoto and Ura in the Spotlight 53
Chapter ⑧②:
Teramoto and Ura-Papa 79
Chapter ⑧③:
Teramoto and the Final Request 105
Chapter ⑧④:
Teramoto and Ura's Alternate Universe 131
Chapter ⑧⑤:
The Girls' School and the Uniform Thief 157
Special Story:
Azuma and Test Cramming Heaven 179

Story: Masahiro Totsuka / Art: Aguri Igarashi

BUILDING: MARTIAL ARTS HALL

ARMOR: AZUMA

宝江高
桑原
宝江高
宝江高
東

CHAPTER 79
THE MUROE HIGH KENDO TEAM AND BURNISH ACADEMY

OOOH!
BAAAN (WHAM)
ARMOR: MIYAZAKI
GYAN (WHANK)
DO !!!

RRRRRR!
GUH!
RRGH!
SFX: PACHI (CLAP) PACHI PACHI
パチパチパチ
YEAH, YOU WERE GREAT.
THAT WAS AMAZING, MIYA-MIYA!
千葉
桑原
NO, I WASN'T !!
THIS SUCKS!!
YOU'RE NOT SUPPOSED TO TAKE OFF YOUR MEN UNTIL YOU SIT DOWN!
宮崎
ARMOR (R-L): CHIBA, KUWAHARA
ISN'T THAT WEIRD!?
OVER AND OVER AND OVER!!
NO MATTER HOW MANY TIMES I TRY, I CAN'T BEAT HER!!
DUHHH...

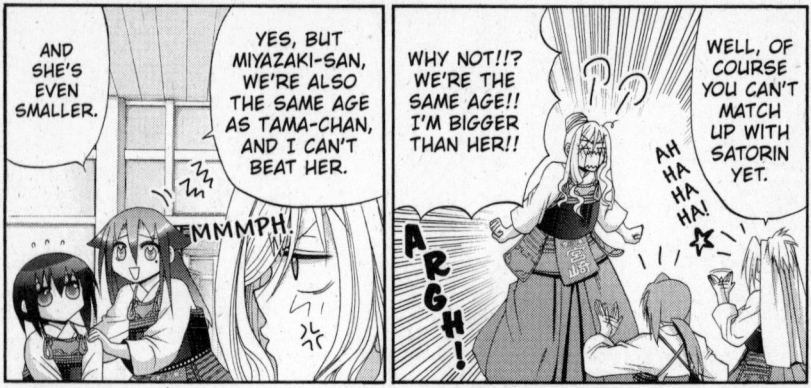

ARMOR (R-L): DOGGY, TAMA

SIX!
MAKING STUFF UP

DAN-KUN!
C'MON, MIYA-MIYA! TRAIN WITH ME!!

...SIX LEVELS, HUH?

ARMOR: EIGA

OH, DAN-KUN... HE'S SCOLDING ME FOR MY OWN SAKE... WHAT A SWEETIE...
AND HE'S BEING HARD ON HIMSELF... WHAT A MAN...

DON'T PUT ON AIRS JUST BECAUSE YOU'VE LEARNED A BIT!
YOU AND I ARE BOTH BEGIN-NERS, AND DON'T FORGET THAT!

HMPH!
BUN
HMPH!
BUN (WHOOSH)
KIRINO, SPEAKING OF THAT KAMASAKI HIGH MEET...

...IT WAS LIKE...
...HE WASN'T THE USUAL KOJIRO-SENSEI WE KNOW.
?

I MEAN, I REALIZE A LOT OF THAT WAS IN COMPARISON TO HOW PATHETIC ISHIBASHI-SENSEI WAS ACTING, BUT...
...DON'T YOU THINK KOJIRO-SENSEI WAS PRETTY COOL THERE?

THAT'S NOT TRUE.
SENSEI'S ALWAYS BEEN LIKE THAT.

校長室
HUH?
SIGN: PRINCIPAL
THAT'S WHAT I SAID, ISHIDA-SENSEI.
TV STATION?

MIIIYAAAKOOO…
…CHAAAAAAAAAN!
ぺっ
ぺっ
ぺっ

BANBUUUU!
(BAMBLOOOSH)
BA
(SPIN)
AAAH! I'M SORRY, TAMA-CHAN!!
.....
UGH, TALK ABOUT CREEPY. YOU NEED TO GET A GRIP AND STOP THINKING ABOUT HER, MIYAKO!
OF COURSE SHE'S NOT. SHE'S JUST BEEN ON MY MIND EVER SINCE I NOTICED THAT SHE DIDN'T SHOW UP AT THE PRACTICE MEET WITH KAMASAKI HIGH.
SHE'S NOT THERE...
HEE
HEE
HEE
FUKI
ふきふき
FUKI
(WIPE)

NO!!
ドギュッ
DOGYU (ZWOOM)
SHE'S HERE!! SHE MUST BE!!
REIMI'S EXACTLY THE KIND OF PERSON WHO'S THERE WHEN YOU THINK SHE ISN'T!!
SFX: JEAA (SWOOSH)
ジェアッ
LOCK THE DOOR, AND SHE'S STUCK OUT THERE!!
BUT I'M NOT LETTING HER IN!!
LOCK
ガチン
GACHIN (CLICK)
バコーン
BAKONNN (WHONNING)
HERE I AM...
AHHH.
WHEW... MUCH BETTER.

ゴゴゴゴ
GOGOGOGOGO (RUMBLE)
クスクスクスクス
RIGHT...
...INSIDE...
クスクスクスクスクスクスゴゴゴゴ
GOGOGO
SFX: KUSU KUSU KUSU KUSU KUSU KUSU KUSU KUSU
SFX: KUSU (GIGGLE) KUSU KUSU
ゴゴゴゴ

ちょこん
CHOKON (PLOP)
HAVE SOME TEA?
IT'S COLD TO SUIT THE HEAT OUTSIDE.
OH, PLEASE DON'T MIND ME.
COLD
KIRINO-SENPAI! DON'T GIVE HER ANY TEA!!
CUP: TEA
YOU WON'T COME AND VISIT ME ANYMORE, MIYAKO-CHAN!
EEK!
GYAAA! DON'T TOUCH ME!
?
WHAT MAKES YOU THINK YOU CAN JUST WALTZ INTO OUR CLUB DOJO, REIMI!!?
さっ
SA (SWISH)
BUT I HAVE TO!
?
RIOT SQUAD
I'VE MISSED YOU SO MUCH, MIYAKO-CHAAAN!
スリスリ
SURI SURI (RUB)
ギュウウウ

I'M ACTUALLY HERE TODAY TO SPEAK WITH EVERYONE, NOT JUST MIYAKO-CHAN.
TV SUNDAY
IS THAT A TV MAGA-ZINE?
WHAT?

TV SUNDAY
BLOW THE RAINY-DAY BLUES AWAY WITH OUR FEATURE ON THIS SEASON'S DRAMAS!
BURNISH ACADEMY

じゃ〜ん
JAAAN (TA-DAA)
BURNISH ACADEMY.
HAVE YOU HEARD OF THIS NEW SHOW?
TV SUNDAY VARIETY
TOTAL FEATURE
CHECK IT OUT! THIS IS AWESOME!
BURNISH ACADEMY SPECIAL!

BURN-ISH ...
... ACA-DEMY ...?
?

YEAH, I'VE SEEN EVERY EPISODE.
I WATCH IT EVERY WEEK!
I'VE GOT EVERY ONE RECORDED!
ワイ
WA!
ワイ
WA! (WHEE!)

ISN'T RYOUKO TODA SUPER-CUTE?
ワイ
WAI (WHEE)
EEEK! EEEEK!
NOT AS MUCH AS ERINA SAWAMIYA!
ワイ
WAI
I'M ON ERINA-CHAN'S SIDE TOO.
?
?
?

WHAT'S FUNNY IS HOW THE HOSTS OF THE SHOW, BURNING DASH, AREN'T EVEN A BIG PART OF IT.
FOR HAVING THEIR NAME IN THE TITLE, NOBODY SEEMS TO CARE IF THEY SHOW UP OR NOT.
?
?

WHOSE TEAM ARE YOU ON, YUJI-KUN? RYOUKO-CHAN OR ERINA-CHAN?
RYOUKO-CHAN'S WAY CUTER!
RIGHT?
HMM... IF I'M BEHIND ANYONE...

...IT WOULD BE MATSU-MOTO, THE AS-SISTANT.
?
?
OOOH! HE LIKES THE OLDER WOMAN!

WHAT ABOUT YOU, TAMA-CHAN?
AH!
UMM...
TV SUNDAY

.....

ARMOR: TAMAKO

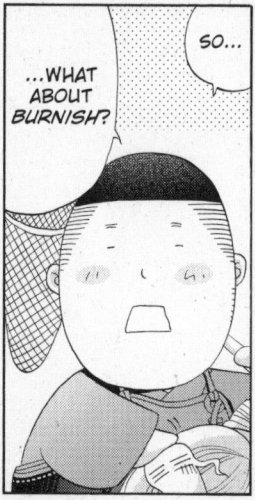

MINE TOO, MINE TOO!
YES! THAT'S MY FAVORITE PART!
SAME FOR ME.
UMM...
YOU KNOW HOW THERE'S THAT SEGMENT OF THE SHOW ABOUT GIRLS WHO ARE ACTIVE IN SPORTS?
...BURNISH SPORTS GIRLS CHEER SQUAD!
SIGN: BURNISH SPORTS GIRLS CHEER SQUAD
OHHHH.
AND BEFORE THAT, IT WAS GIRLS' SOCCER.
IT SHOWED HOW SHE ROUNDED UP OTHER MEMBERS AND EVENTUALLY WON A GAME IN A TOURNAMENT.
LAST TIME THEY COVERED A GIRLS' BASKETBALL TEAM WITH ONLY ONE MEMBER.
SFX: GABA (LURCH)
WHAT DO YOU THINK YOU'RE DOING!?
...SENT THEM A PICTURE OF MIYAKO-CHAN.
WELL, I, REIMI ODAJIMA...
WHAT!!?
MANAGER

...OKAME TV, SAYING THEY WANT TO COME SEE THE TEAM!
HEE HEEE!
AND THEN, WHO SHOULD I GET A CALL FROM BUT...
HUH!?

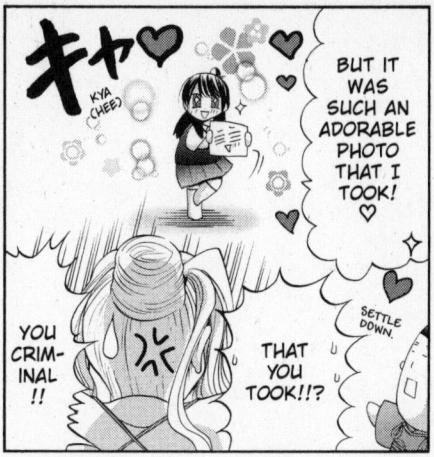
キャ
KYA (HEE)
BUT IT WAS SUCH AN ADORABLE PHOTO THAT I TOOK!
SETTLE DOWN.
YOU CRIM-INAL!!
THAT YOU TOOK!!?

ACTUALLY, IT APPEARS TO BE TRUE.

WOW! SO THEY WANT TO PUT OUR CLUB ON TV!?
BUT THAT'S INCREDIBLE!!
I DON'T KNOW IF I BUY THIS...

KOJIRO-SENSEI!
MIND UNLOCKING THE DOOR FOR ME?

ALBUM: BEAUTY

PAPERS: SIGNUP

HUH? BETWEEN ERINA SAWAMIYA AND RYOUKO TODA?
BY THE WAY, WHOSE TEAM ARE YOU ON, SENSEI?
BROMIDE
BROMIDE
RYOUKO-CHAN, RIGHT!?
SHOULDN'T THAT BE OBVIOUS?
WE'RE COMPLETELY FOR IT!!
AND THAT STARTS WITH ASKING YOUR OPINION.
WE GET TO MEET ERINA-CHAN AND RYOUKO-CHAN, RIGHT!?
ARMOR (R-L): CHIBA, KUWAHARA
Ryouko Toda, age seven-teen!
This cool, intelligent actress burst into the nation's living rooms when she played the heroine in last year's hit drama, *Kiyomura-san and Suginokouji-san*!!
Erina Sawa-miya, age six-teen!
A promising new talent who made a big splash with her commercial this spring!!

NOTEBOOK: KIRINOTES, TOP SECRET.

ARMOR: TEAM RYOUKO ARMOR: TEAM ERINA

THAT'S RIGHT! I AM TERAMOTO, SUPERVISOR OF THE TOURYUU ACADEMY KENDO TEAM!
YES!

TOU-RYUU ACAD-EMY, KYU-SHU

I... UNDER-STAND...
...YES...

YES, I SENT IT!
ざわ
ZAWA (MURMUR)
THAT'S CORRECT!
ざわ
ZAWA
YES!
YES!

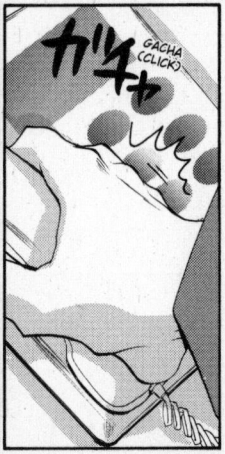
ガチャ
GACHA (CLICK)

SAKAKI!
I'VE GOTTEN A TELEVISION OFFER ABOUT YOU.
FROM OKAME TV!!
ZAN (ZSHH)

BAMBOO BLADE

バンブーブレード

BAMBOO BLADE
バンブーブレード

わい
WAI
わい
WAI
調理実習室
わい
WAI (WHEE)
SIGN: HOME ECONOMICS
WHAT, HOME EC!? CAN I HAVE SOME? FOR ME? ME? SOME? FOR ME?
I GUESS I'D BETTER SAVE SOME OF THIS...
...TO TAKE TO KOJIRO-SENSEI.
OH, WHAT A BOTHER.
ばーん
BAAN (TA-DAA)
ALL DONE!
IS THE KENDO TEAM GONNA BE ON BURNISH ACADEMY!?
わらわら
WARA WARA (SQUISH)
HEY KIRINO, IS IT TRUE? IS IT TRUE?
SHAMOJI
WE DON'T KNOW THAT YET...
...SO DON'T GET YOUR HOPES UP.
ワイ
WAI
OH! SO IT IS TRUE!
I DON'T BELIEVE IT! YOU'RE GONNA BE ON TV?
HOW PUZZLING...
HUH? WHERE WOULD YOU HEAR SOME-THING LIKE THAT?
ワイ
WAI

CHAPTER 80
TV AND COMMERCIALS

どや
DOYA
1-9
DOYA (MURMUR)
どや
HEE-HEE-HEE
DID YOU BRING IT?
IN A GOOD MOOD
KAWAZOE-SAAAN!
YES.
ANIME DVD
ドドドド
DODODO (STAMPEDE)
KAWA-ZOE-SAN!!
WOWWW, THANK YOU SO MUCH.
HEE HEE!..
I'LL LET YOU BORROW MY FAVORITE SOMETIME SOON!!
WE SHOULD HANG OUT AT MY HOUSE AND WATCH IT!!

TAMA IS STARTLED BY THE SUDDEN ONRUSH OF CLASSMATES WHO USUALLY DON'T GIVE HER THE TIME OF DAY.
MEOW!
BUT WHY...?
YEAH.
ワイワイ
WAI
WAI (WHEE)
YOU'RE IN THE KENDO CLUB, RIGHT?
WE DON'T KNOW YET...
IS IT TRUE THAT BURNISH IS COMING TO COVER OUR KENDO TEAM!?
YEAH.
CAN WE COME AND WATCH THE FILMING?
I HOPE THEY BRING THE CAMERAS ON CAMPUS!
FINALLY, A BIT OF GLORY FOR THIS BORING SCHOOL!!
WOW!! I HOPE OUR SCHOOL IS ON TV!!
きゃあ
KYAA (EEEK)
IF IT'S ON TV, I'LL WATCH IT!!
きゃあ
KYAA
WE'RE ALL ROOTING FOR YOU!
GOOD LUCK, KAWA-ZOE-SAN!

.....
THANKS.
ワイワイ
WAI
WAI
WAI
WAI
(WHEE)
HEH HEH!
JUST BETWEEN US GIRLS, OKAY?
YOU CAN'T TELL ANYONE ELSE.
NOTHING'S BEEN FINALIZED, SEE?
I MEAN, THIS IS A TV APPEARANCE WE'RE TALKING ABOUT! THEY'LL BE COMING TO FILM OUR KENDO TEAM!
WAI
WAI
ワイワイ
GAYA
GAYA (YAMMER)
がやがや

バーン
BAAN (BOOM)
I AM, AFTER ALL, AN INDIS-PENSABLE MEMBER OF THE TEAM!
THAT'S SO COOOOL!
HOOO-HO-HO-HO!!
I SUPPOSE I DON'T HAVE A CHOICE!
WOW, SENPAI! YOU'RE GONNA BE ON TV?
はっ
HA (GASP)
ギギギ
SFX: GIGIGI (CREAK)
SHA
シャッ
SHA (SHING)
シャッ
GET BACK HERE!
...THE LITTLE PIGGY SQUEALING ALL OF OUR SECRETS.
I THINK I FOUND...
SURARI (SWISH)
すらり

DON (BAM)
ドン
HEY!
DON
ドンドン
DON
YOUR FOOT-WORK'S GOTTEN REALLY GOOD, DAN-KUN.
I KNOW, RIGHT?
シュタシュタ
SHUTA
SHUTA (HOP)
WHEW!
ガラッ
GARA (CLUNK)
THIS THING'S HEAVY!
ドンドン
DON
DON
SOME-ONE! OPEN THE DOOR!
COM-ING!
THAT'S KOJIRO-SENSEI.
...A LITTLE BIT OF BURNISH ACADEMY.
ポン
PON (PAT)
WELL, BOYS, WE'RE GONNA SIT DOWN AND WATCH...
WHAT'S WITH THE TV?
ドン
DON (THUMP)

DO YOU THINK SATOREEM WILL REMEMBER?
I HOPE...
BUT AZUMA SAYS SHE RECORDS IT EVERY WEEK, SO SHE'LL BRING IT IN.
EVEN MIYA HERSELF HASN'T SEEN THE SHOW.
I'VE NEVER ACTUALLY SAT DOWN TO WATCH THE SHOW.
SAME WITH TAMA.
YEAH, I'LL BET SHE GETS IT CONFUSED WITH SOMETHING ELSE AND BRINGS HER GAME GEAR ON ACCIDENT.
HMMM...
YEAH, THAT'S WHAT I'M WORRIED ABOUT.
AZUMA-SAN!
OHO!
NOT TODAY, FELLOWS!!
ザッ
ZA (ZSHH)
じゃーん
JAAAN (TA-DAAA)
OOOOH!
...I'VE BROUGHT THE GOODS!!
ON A VHS TAPE! IN THIS DAY AND AGE?
AS YOU CAN SEE...
ふっふっふっ! HEH-HEH-HEH!
LOOK.

WRITING: BURNISH ACADEMY VIDEO

ZA (ZSHH)
MIYA-MIYA!
THAT REIMI AND HER MEDDLING!
LOOKS LIKE SHE DOESN'T MIND IT TO ME.
SHE'S GUNG HO!
FASAAA (FWOOSH)
TALK ABOUT A BOTHER.
YAAAAY!
LET'S WATCH THE SHOW!
EVERYONE HERE?

TELEVISION TITLE: BURNISH ACADEMY

WHAT DO YOU MEAN, KIRINO?
OH, IF ONLY I COULD BE CUTE LIKE THEM...
YOU'RE PLENTY CUTE!
WELL, THEY'RE BOTH SUPER-CUTE.
I'M NOT GIVIN' HER UP!
BUT I'M STILL IN RYOUKO TODA-CHAN'S CAMP!
やったぁ YAAAY!
ぱやぁぁぁ
OF COURSE! WHO ELSE WOULD OFFER ME FREE ORANGE TARTS!?
REALLY, KOJIRO-SENSEI?
SFX: PAYAAA (GLOW)
ARE YOU KIDDING? ABSO-LUTELY!
AND US?
YOU'RE CUTE AS WELL, SAYA!
SENSEI! WHAT ABOUT ME? WHAT ABOUT ME?
NADE
NADE (RUB)
なでなで

HA HA HA HA HA!!

EVERY GIRL ON MY TEAM IS A BONA FIDE CUTIE-PIE!!

CUP: TEA

TELEVISION: OKAME MYSTERY THEATER: OCHUGEN COP

AHA! THIS IS THE PART!
ババーン♪
BABAAAN (DADAA)
I CAN LIST ALL THE SPELLS IN MATERIAL PUZZLE FROM MEMORY!!
BUT I CAN SAY THE FULL NAMES OF EVERY CHARACTER WHO APPEARS IN BLADE BRAVER...!!
TELEVISION: BURNISH SPORTS GIRLS CHEER SQUAD
スポ魂少女
応援団
ハジャーン
HAJAAAN (YADAAA)
AND THEY WANT TO HAVE MIYA-MIYA ON THIS SECTION, HUH?
SEE?
THEY MOSTLY COVER MIDDLE AND HIGH SCHOOLERS.
IT'S A SEGMENT THAT FOCUSES ON GIRLS IN SPORTS.
OHHH.

THEY GO RIGHT TO THE SCHOOL AND FILM THEM BUSY AT PRACTICE...
...OR CALL THEM TO THE STUDIO AND HAVE THEM COMPETE AGAINST OTHER SCHOOLS OR CELEBRITIES.
IT'S A VERY FREE-FORM SEGMENT. THEY DO THINGS WHICHEVER WAY THEY WANT.

NUUUN CLOOMO
WELL, YOU CAN'T SEE A GIRL'S FACE WITH A MEN COVERING IT UP.
THAT'S NOT AS FUN FOR THE TV AUDIENCE.
OH, GOOD POINT.

AND NOW THEY'RE COVERING KENDO GIRLS?
WILL THAT WORK ON TV?
WHY NOT?

SFX: GURU (SPIN) GURU

HO-HO-HO!
...entitled *Piercing Love*, this summer.
Chiyoko-san will be starring in a feature film...
ANOTHER AD?
ワー
WAAA (RAHHH)
...legendary actress Chiyoko Ueda!
Here's our next guest...
Hello everyone.
KYAAA (EEEEK)
キャーッ
IS IT JUST ME...
Pierce!
Haaaa!!
DOUN (BOOM)
Piercing Love! In theaters this July...
...OR ARE THESE ADS MULTIPLYING?
7月公開
愛をつらぬけ
THIS SHOW IS ALL ABOUT THE ADS.
TELEVISION: COMING THIS JULY—PIERCING LOVE
HUH?
We, Burning Dash, have one last message to you guys...
Time to say good-bye, folks!
That's all for this week!
WAI
ワイ
WAI (WHEE)
ワイ

SIGN: BURNING CRASH

SFX: MOGYU (MUNCH) MOGYU

SFX: MARTIAL ARTS HALL

SIGN: FACULTY ROOM

PLEASE REFUSE.
COMING TO COVER ME?
A TV STATION?
...ON THE SWORD.
I HAVE GIVEN UP...
THE TIMES, THEY ARE A-CALLING... FOR YOU!
YES, BURNISH ACADEMY? WE ACCEPT YOUR OFFER.
I'M AFRAID YOU DON'T HAVE A CHOICE, SAKAKI.
HELLO?

BAMBOO BLADE

バンブーブレード

BAMBOO BLADE
バンブーブレード

FUKUOKA, KYUSHU
MARINE MESSE FUKUOKA

SIGN: MARINE MESSE FUKUOKA

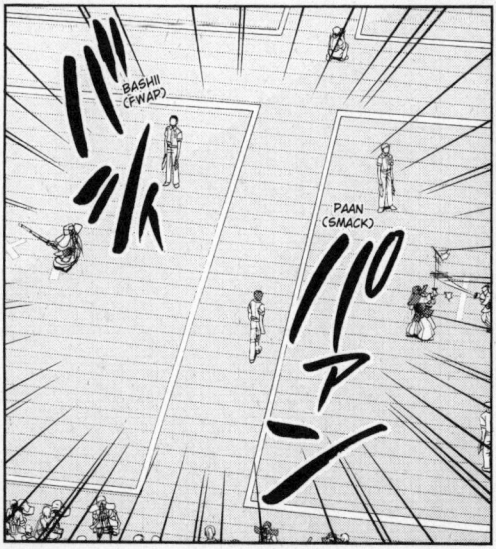

SIGN: GYOKURYUUKI

BEGIN!
スッ
SU (SWISH)
スッ
SU
本間
ARMOR: HONMA
ARMOR: TOURYUU ACADEMY
バコッ
BAKO (WHAP)
KYEH!
バン
BAN (WHAM)
KIEEE!

SIGN: GIRLS' KENDO MEET

DOOO!!!
ONE YEAR AGO

CHAPTER 81
TERAMOTO AND URA IN THE SPOTLIGHT

AND THEY DIDN'T EVEN SCORE A POINT ON HER!
ZAWA (MURMUR)
TOU-RYUU'S SENPO JUST WON THE ENTIRE MATCH ON HER OWN!

OO (COUGH)
SHE BEAT ALL FIVE!!

PLUS...
...SHE'S A FIRST-YEAR.

...ALL ON HER OWN...
ZAWA
ZAWA
AGAINST THE MIGHTY OOKUMA HIGH...
ZAWA

A FIRST-YEAR STUDENT!

HA HA! HA
GEEZ, YOU COULDN'T LEAVE ANY FOR US?
NICE WORK, SAKAKI-SAN.
ペコ
PEKO (BOW)
ドッキ
DOKKI
ドッキ
DOKKI (BA-BUMP)
ドヨ
DOYO (MURMUR)
THE NEWEST WEAPON OF TOURYUU ACADEMY ...
桃竜学院
榊
...URA SAKAKI!
ARMOR: TOURYUU ACADEMY – SAKAKI

SECOND ROUND!
PAAN (THWACK)
DOON (BOOM)

ARMOR: SAKAKI
THAT MAKES TEN!!!
榊

I DIDN'T WANT TO BELIEVE IT.
ハア
HAA
ハア
HAA
ハア
HAA
I USED TO HATE THE WORD "GENIUS." I NEVER BELIEVED IN IT.
ARMOR: TERAMOTO
AND MY BODY DID INDEED REMEMBER THE MOVES, MY REFLEXES HONED AND SENSES SHARPENED.
WHEN I WAS YOUNG, I THOUGHT THAT WITH PRACTICE, YOU COULD REACH ANY LEVEL OF SKILL.
ハア
HAA (HUFF)
BUT...
ハア
HAA
THIRD ROUND!

I FOUND OTHERS THAT NO AMOUNT OF PRACTICE WOULD HELP ME BEAT.
...I HIT A WALL.
I HAD AN EPIPHANY.
PAAN (WHACK)
桃巻学院
...THERE ARE SOME SO POWERFUL THAT THEY ARE EFFECTIVELY OUT OF REACH.
BUT IT'S STRANGE...
PRACTICE WILL INDEED IMPROVE ONE'S SKILLS.
ARMOR: TOURYUU ACADEMY - SAKAKI
BISHI! (WHAP)
桃巻学院
...THAT THIS WAS PROOF OF INNATE "TALENT."
I DID NOT WANT TO ADMIT...

ARMOR: HASHIMOTO

SIGN: MARINE MESSE FUKUOKA

FIFTEEN IN A ROW!
THAT MAKES FIFTEEN!
OVER-WHELMING TALENT.

I WAS ABSOLUTELY FLATTENED.
ドッキン
DOKKIN (BA-BUMP)
ドッキン
DOKKIN
ハア
HAA (HUFF)
ハア
HAA
ドッキン
DOKKIN
ハア
HAA
...HAD ME HEAD OVER HEELS.
ドッキン
DOKKIN
ハア
HAA
ドッキン
DOKKIN
ドッキン
DOKKIN
ドッキン
DOKKIN
ハア
HAA
THE VERY NATURE OF HER BRIL-LIANCE...
IT CANNOT BE FOUND IN THESE MERE PLACES.
...DOES NOT EXIST IN VICTORY, LOSS, OR PERSONAL IMPROVEMENT.
GENIUS—TRUE GENIUS...
SUCH BEAUTY.
THE BEAUTY.

桃竜学院
榊
ARMOR: TOURYUU ACADEMY - SAKAKI
TRUE GENIUS...

...THAT IS ENTIRELY DIFFER-ENT FROM OURS.
...EXISTS BENEATH A SUN...
神

DO YOUR BEST OUT THERE.

THIRD DAY OF THE MEET

WHAT IS IT, SAKAKI?
IS SOME-THING WRONG?
NO...
NOTHING.

.....
BEGIN!

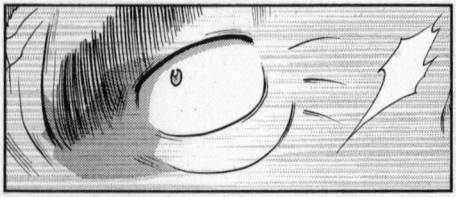

FOURTH ROUND!

バシッ
BASHI (SMACK)
ARMOR: SAKAKI
ザワ
ZAWA (MUIRMUIR)
SHE WAS SCORED UPON...
SAKAKI-SAN!
ビシッ
BISHII (FWAPP)
THERE'S ANOTHER ONE.
KOTE!
TH-THIS CAN'T BE HAPPENING...!!
S...
SA-KAKI ...?

ARMOR: SAKAKI

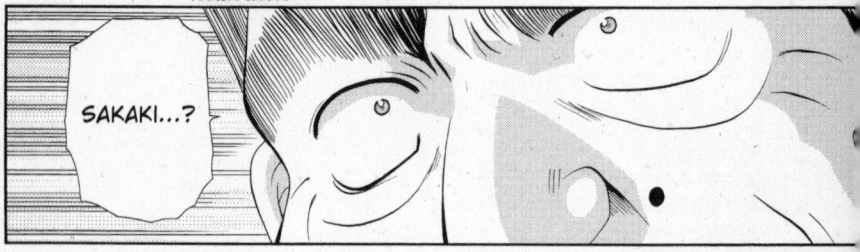

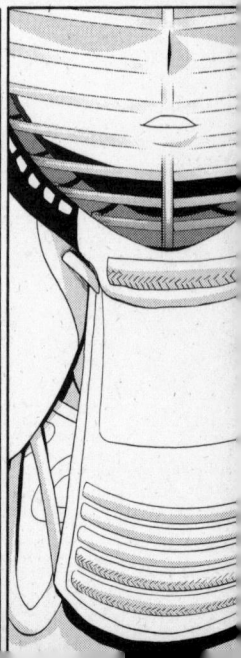

PAN (WHACK)
パン
PAAN
パアン
BANNER: INVINCIBLE ARMADA
SIGN: GRACEFUL AS THE CRANE
AND FROM THAT POINT ON...
...URA SAKAKI NEVER SET FOOT IN THE TRAINING HALL OF THE TOURYUU ACADEMY KENDO TEAM AGAIN.

SIGN: SWEETS TSURUYA

SIGN: SAKAKI

SFX: PINPORON (DINGLE-DONG)

WELCOME TO MY HUMBLE ABODE, COACH TERA-MOTO!!

ギッ
GI (CREAK)

I SEE!!

I HAVE COME TO DISCUSS YOUR DAUGHTER, SIR.

BATAN (THUMP)
バタン

PLEASE, COME INSIDE.
THANK YOU.

MUROE HIGH
IT'S NOT A DONE DEAL YET!
WHAT DID I TELL YOU PEOPLE?
WAI (WHEE)
I'M GONNA GET TO SHAKE RYOUKO-CHAN'S HAND!
ワイワイ
WAI
I'M GONNA GET ME ERINA-CHAN'S AUTO-GRAPH!
MY ENTIRE CLASS ASKED ME TO GET AUTOGRAPHS...
AND I'LL TAKE A PICTURE!
AUTOGRAPH SHEET
FASSAAA (SWOOSH)
ファッサァ〜♥

BAMBOO BLADE

バンブーブレード

BAMBOO BLADE
バンブーブレード

TOKYO

IS THIS REALLY THE SAME TOKYO?
HOW CAN THIS BE...?
... NO ...
.....
CURSE THEM ...!!
THIS IS ALL THAT DEMONIC DEVIL ARMY'S WORK...!
TOKYO REJECTED ME... AND NOW IT'S REAPIN' ITS REWARDS!!
IT AIN'T MY PROB-LEM WHAT HAPPENS TO TOKYO ...
NO, I DON'T CARE WHAT HAPPENS TO OTHER HUMAN BEINGS.

クルッ
KURU (SPIN)
スタッ
SUTA (STOMP)
YAAH!
SHUBAAA (LEAP)
!!
ドオンズーン
DOON ZUUUN (BOOM BMMM)
THE DEMONIC DEVIL ARMY IS CLOSE AT HAND!!
THEY'RE HERE!!
ピピー
PIPIII (BEEBEEP)
ピー
PIII
カチ
KACHI
KACHI
KACHI
パカ
PAKA (FLIP)
シャキ
SHAKI (SHKING)

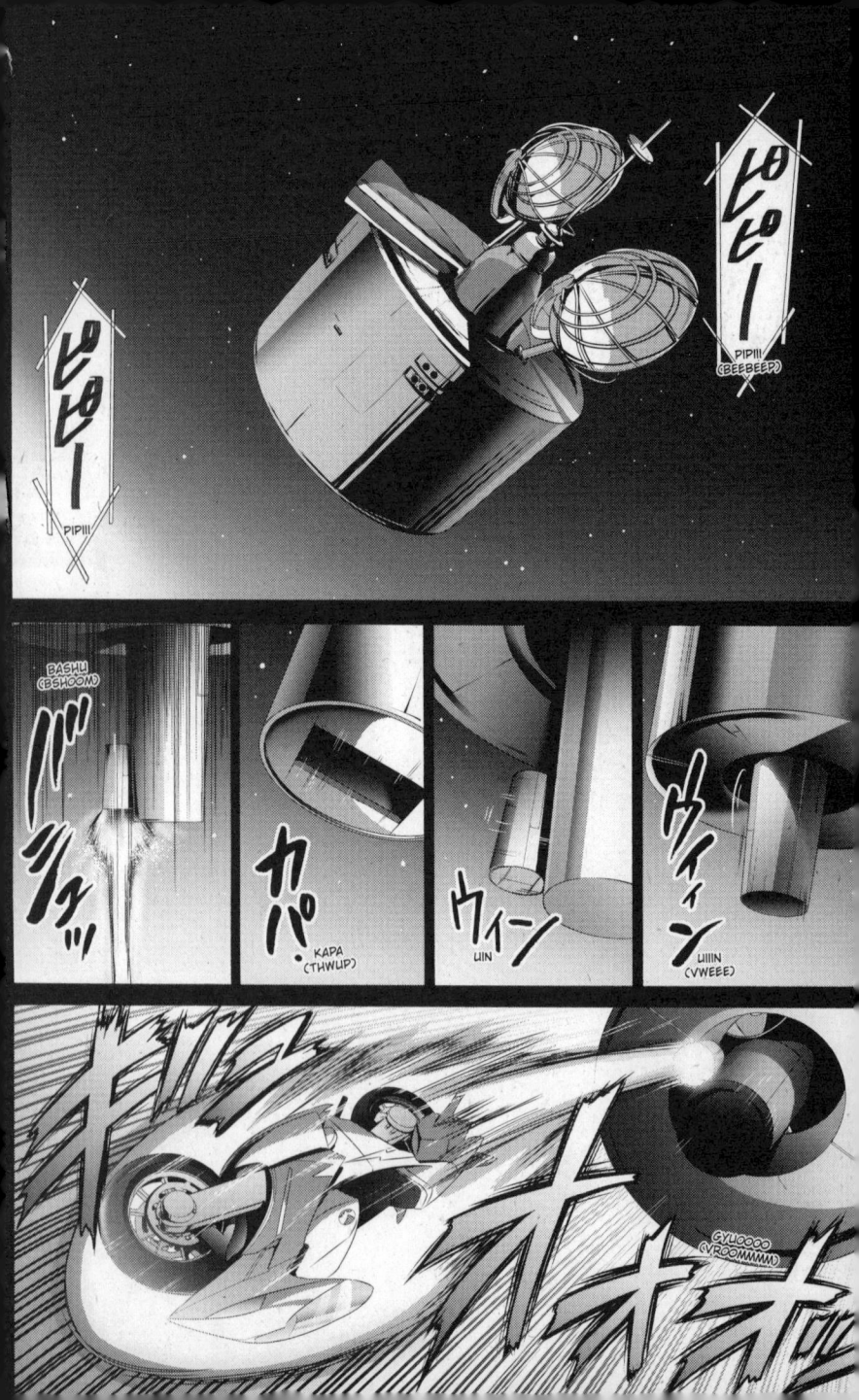
ピピー
PIPIII
(BEEPBEEP)
ピピー
PIPIII
BASHU
(BSHOOM)
バシュッ
カパ
KAPA
(THWUP)
ウィーン
UIIN
ウィィィン
UIIIIN
(VWEEE)
キュゴゴゴ
(VROOMMMM)

GYUOOOOO
GYUOO
OOOOO (OOOMM)
BASHU (BSHHHKK)
SHUUUU (HSSSS)
DON (WHAM)

DORUN
DORUN
DO (PUTT)
DO
DO
DO
DORUN (VRMM)
GARU (GRMM)
DOONN (BOOOM)
MOVE OUT!
KYUIIIIIN (SCREEEE)
DURAN BIKE!!

キイイイイイイイイイ
KIIIIIIIII (VREEEE)
(EEEEEE)
BA (ZOOM)
ドッドッドッ
DO DO DO
GYAGYA (SHRIEEEK)
ギャギャ!!
THEY'VE COMPLETED IT...!!
D-DEAR GOD...

TOWERING TOWER!!
GOGOGOGO GOGO (GOOMMM)
HE'S HERE! HE MUST BE!!
DO
DO
DO (SPLITT)
KAISER EMPEROR!!
THE TIME FOR THE FINAL BATTLE IS AT HAND!!
TIME TO RIDE UP THERE!
KAAA!
KAAA!
ZA (LEAP)
ZA
!!

KAAA!
ZA
ZA
KAAA!
THEY SPOTTED ME!!
DAMN!
JAKI (CHUNK)
JAKI
TRANS-FORM!
VAAAAN (VWAAAAN)
AAAAA (VWAAAA)
KAAAA (FLASH)

BLACK DURAN!!!!

CHAPTER 82
TERAMOTO AND URA-PAPA

OH, DON'T MIND ME!
コト。
KOTO (TINK)
PLEASE!
...SO I CAN ONLY DO SO MUCH FOR A GUEST.
カチャ。
KACHA (CLINK)
HA HA
I'M AFRAID MY WIFE IS AWAY ON VACATION AT THE MOMENT...
GOODNESS!
7
日 月 火 水 木 金 土
HOW-EVER...
YES. THE TEAM IS BUSY TRAINING FOR THE MEET.
GI (CREAK)
ギッ
IT'S NEARLY TIME FOR GYOKURYUUKI AGAIN.
...IF I MAY BE FRANK, IT WILL BE DIFFICULT TO WIN WITH-OUT YOUR DAUGHTER.

I DON'T KNOW WHY SHE QUIT KENDO...
HAA (SIGH)
はあ~
BUT AS ASHAMED AS I AM TO ADMIT THIS, EVEN I DON'T UNDERSTAND IT.
I'M VERY SORRY ABOUT ALL THE TROUBLE.
HA HA
ずず...
ZUZU (SIP)
...IS FEELING THE EMPTINESS THAT COMES FROM THE LACK OF A PROPER RIVAL.
SPEAKING AS A TEACHER AND KENDO INSTRUCTOR...
...I BELIEVE YOUR DAUGHTER...

SHE HAS NO REAL FOES HER AGE.
THERE ARE NO GIRLS IN HIGH SCHOOL THAT CAN MATCH URA.
INDEED...
SO YOU AGREE, SENSEI?
SHE HAS MASTERED HER REALM AND LOST HER REASON TO FIGHT.
THAT WAS MY GUESS AS WELL.

THOUGH I SHOULD NOT SPEAK SO HIGHLY OF MY OWN DAUGHTER, I'M AFRAID THAT URA...
...HAS TOO MUCH TALENT.
SHE HAS GROWN TOO FAST.
...I BELIEVE SHE HAS BURNED OUT ALREADY.
.....
BURNED OUT...
AND THOSE WHO HAVE BURNED OUT...
... THEY ...
...DO NOT COME BACK TO US...

SFX: KOPOPOPOPOPO (BLUP BLUP)

MMM!?
THE GIRL FROM THE KANSAI AREA, CORRECT? SHE WAS THE ONLY ONE WHO MATCHED URA.
SPEAKING OF YAMADA, I WONDER WHAT HAPPENED TO HER.
SHE MUST HAVE BEEN SO BORED...
.....
AND IT TURNS OUT... SHE QUIT KENDO TOO.
しおしお
TEA
I ASKED YAMADA'S MIDDLE SCHOOL INSTRUCTOR TO SEE WHAT SHE'S BEEN UP TO.
THAT'S RIGHT! I WAS CURIOUS, SO I LOOKED HER UP!
GATA (THUMP)
SFX: SHIO (WILT) SHIO
I SUPPOSE THAT MUST HAPPEN WITH EVERY GIRL SOONER OR LATER!!
THAT IS SOOO NOT WITH IT.
LAMERS!
NAH, LIKE, KENDO IS SO, LIKE, SMELLY AND DUMB?
FUZZY FAN
LIKE, OMGGD?
KU...!! (SOB)
AFTER SHE REACHED HIGH SCHOOL, SHE SEEMS TO HAVE TURNED SHALLOW AND COMPLETELY CHANGED HER PERSONALITY!!
AN OLD MAN'S IMAGINATION

IT IS A DIFFICULT TOPIC...!!
I DON'T UNDERSTAND...! I JUST DON'T UNDERSTAND GIRLS!!
BUN
BUN (WHOOSH)
GABAA (LUNGE)
BOO HOO HOO!
UNEXPLAINED LIFE-FORMS!
ALAS! OH, THE TRAGEDY...!!
BUHHAA (BLOOSH)
ARMOR: DUDE
ARMOR: MAN
ONLY BECAUSE THEY'RE SO SIMPLE-MINDED...
I WALK THE PATH OF BATTLE!
I'M GONNA BE BETTER THAN YOU!
THINK OF HOW EASY IT IS TO WORK WITH BOYS BY COMPARISON...
YOU'RE TOUGH! CAN'T WAIT TO FIGHT YOU AGAIN!
I JUST WANNA BE STRONG!!!
I WAS BORN TO FIGHT AGAINST YOU!
LET ME SHOW YOU MY NEW MOVE!
HA HA HA

...I THOUGHT WE MIGHT CALL UPON THE HELP OF TELEVISION.
OHHH!
BURNISH ACADEMY, YOU MEAN?

THERE IS NOTHING MORE IN OUR POWER TO DO.
ON THE OTHER HAND, IF YOU DON'T MIND...

MEANING THAT IF YOU SUGGEST IT AS PART OF A TV SHOW, SHE'LL BE UNABLE TO REFUSE THE OPPORTUNITY!
BRILLIANT!
BUT NOT ONLY THAT, SIR!

THAT WOULD HAVE BEEN ANOTHER CHANCE TO BE ON TV!
YES, OF COURSE!
I REMEMBER!
GIRLS' KENDO ENJOYED A BIT OF PRESTIGE AT THE TIME, IF YOU RECALL.

DO YOU REMEMBER THE SHOW *KENDO KOMACHI*?
OF COURSE! "KENDO TOWN"!
HAVEN'T HEARD THE NAME IN AGES!
WAI (WHEE)
WAI
わいわい

THEY HELD A SPECIAL EPISODE FEATURING THE MANY POWERFUL AND BEAUTIFUL FEMALE STUDENTS ACTIVE IN THE KENDO WORLD, SUCH AS YOUR DAUGHTER.
AS YOU RECALL, THEY WANTED TO INTRODUCE MIGHTY AND GLAMOROUS GIRLS FROM ALL OVER JAPAN.
IN THE END, THEY HAD NINE GIRLS, INCLUDING YAMADA FROM KANSAI AND SUZUKI FROM TOKYO.
AND OF COURSE ...
GOGOGOGO (RUMBLE)
...THERE WERE PLENTY OF GIRLS WHO WEREN'T SHOWN ON *KENDO KOMACHI* WHO HAD PLENTY OF STRENGTH BUT NOT SO MUCH OF THE BEAUTY...
IN SECRET, THEY WERE NICKNAMED ***THE BIG BRUTES.***
ALAS! THE POOR GIRLS...
SOB!
SOB!

IN ORDER TO BRING YOUR DAUGHTER BACK TO KENDO, SHE WILL NEED A RIVAL.
THESE ARE THE GIRLS WHO FIT THE BILL!!
THE NINE CHOSEN FOR *KENDO KOMACHI* HAVE ALREADY DEVELOPED RIVALRIES WITH EACH OTHER!
BUT MOST OF ALL, THEY SEEK TO DEFEAT URA SAKAKI!!
UNLIKE YOUR DAUGHTER WHO'S TAKEN A BREAK FROM KENDO, THESE GIRLS HAVE CONTINUED THEIR TRAINING!
IF THEY FOUGHT NOW, URA-SAN'S VICTORY WOULD NOT BE ASSURED!!
WAIT, COACH TERA-MOTO.
YOU WANT TO SEND NOT ONLY MY DAUGHTER TO *BURNISH ACADEMY*, BUT THE *KENDO KOMACHI* GIRLS AS WELL?
THAT IS RIGHT!!

I WILL CALL UPON THE POWER OF TELEVISION...
神

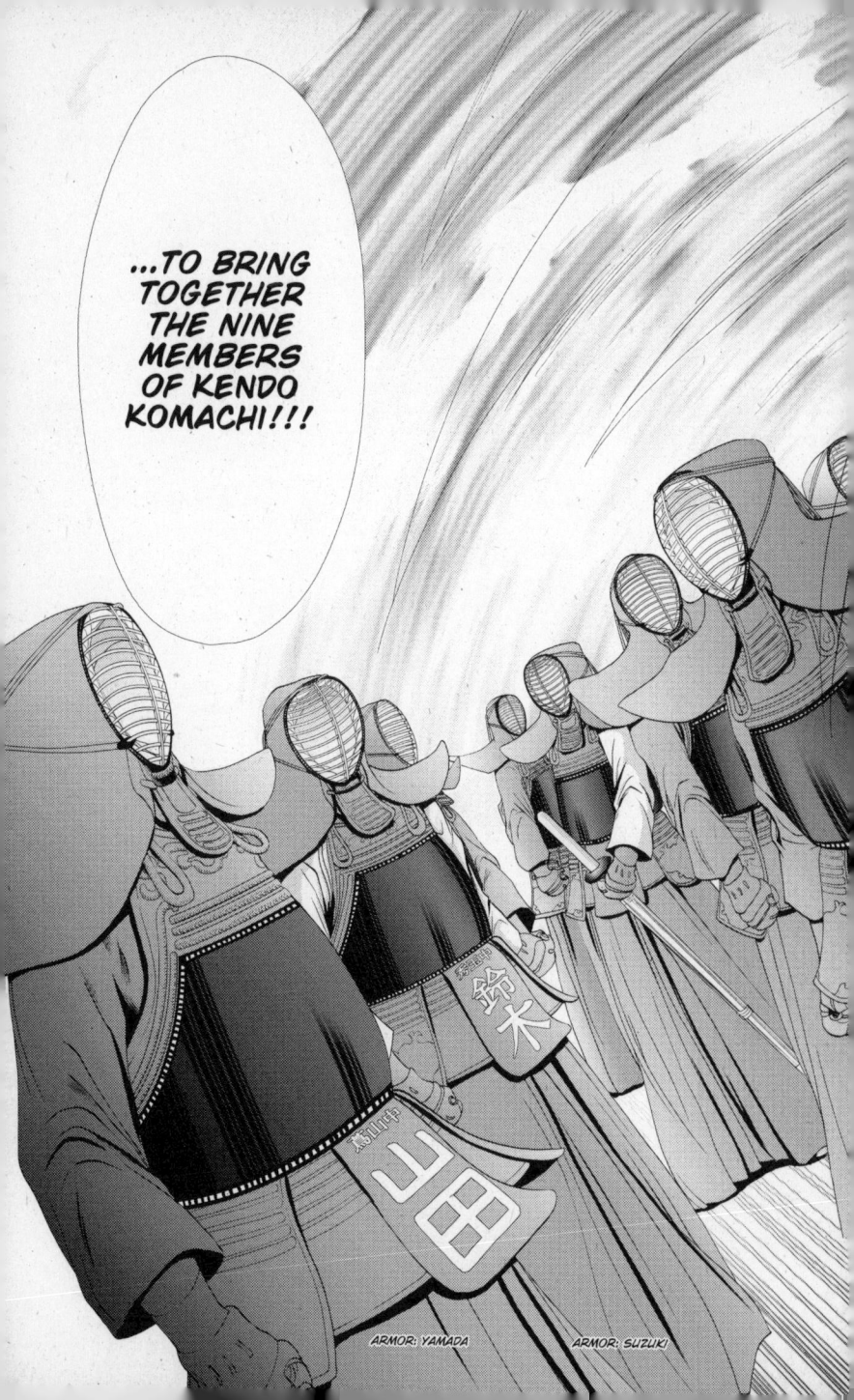
...TO BRING TOGETHER THE NINE MEMBERS OF KENDO KOMACHI!!!
鈴木
山田
ARMOR: YAMADA
ARMOR: SUZUKI

...THAT THIS PLAN IS CERTAIN TO BRING YOUR DAUGHTER BACK INTO THE FOLD.
I BELIEVE...
I'M HOME.

BAMBOO BLADE

バンブーブレード

BAMBOO BLADE
バンブーブレード

KAAAAA (FLASH)
カアアアア
DURAN SWORD!!!
DODODODO (ZIZNNNNO)
KAAA!
KAAA!
RAAHHH!
DOSHU (DSHH)
GYUUOOO (VRRNNNNO)
ZUBAA (SLICE)
ZUBAA

BON (BOOM)
BON
KAAAAA!
BOON
!!
KIIIIII (SCREEEE)
GOTTA KEEP GOING!!
BARI (VRMM)
BARI
SO, YOU HAVE COME, BLACK DURAN.
COME TO YOUR DOOM, THAT IS!!

COUNT BARON!!
BASAA (FLAP)
PREPARE YOURSELF!!
RAHHHH!!
GAKIIN (CLANG)
TOP FLOOR OF TOWERING TOWER
ALMOST TIME...
IT IS ALMOST TIME FOR EVERYTHING TO COME TO AN END.
KAISER'S CHAMBER
KAISER EMPEROR

AFTER TWO HUNDRED LONG YEARS, MY GREATEST WISH IS FINALLY COMING TO FRUITION.
KA (TOKK)
THE HUMAN EXTINCTION AND EARTH PURIFICATION PLAN!!!
I WILL WIPE OUT ALL OF THE FOOLISH HUMANS AND PURIFY THIS PLANET.
BUT HIS LIFE ENDS TODAY!!
BASAA (FLAP)
THE ONLY REMAINING OBSTACLE IS BLACK DURAN.
KNIGHT OF NIGHT!!
BARI
BARI
BARI
BARI
BARI (ZZAP)
HEED MY CALL!!
CRUSH THE LIFE FROM BLACK DURAN ONCE AND FOR ALL!!
GO FORTH!!
SHUUUUUU (FSHHH)

DON (WHAM)
HA-HA-HA-HA-HA!
BRING THIS PLANET BACK TO THE FORM IT HELD UPON ITS BIRTH!!
ONCE YOU HAVE DONE THAT, SLAUGHTER THE HUMANS THAT DEFILE THIS WORLD!!
WHA...?
TIME FOR YOU TO STEP ASIDE.
NOW IT'S MY TIME.
YOU'VE AGED ...
... OLD MAN.
KNIGHT OF NIGHT ...
... WHAT HAVE YOU ...?

AHH!
ダダダダダ
DADADADADA (RUSH)
SO IT'S YOU AND ME, IS IT?
KNIGHT OF NIGHT!!
!!
WAIT...
W...
SU (SWISH)
STILL ALIVE, COUNT BARON?
...NOT FINISHED YET...
I'M...
YORO (WOBBLE)
THERE YOU ARE, BLACK DU-RAN...

WING SLASH!!
AAAAAGH!
DOGOOOO (KABOOOM)
OOOOO (FSHHHH)
.....
DON'T INTER-FERE...
I'VE NEVER SEEN IT THAT WAY.
WHY WOULD YOU DO THAT?
HE WAS YOUR FRIEND! HE WAS ON YOUR SIDE!!
FRIEND...?
EVERY-THING IN THIS WORLD IS MERELY A TOOL THAT I CAN USE TO MY BENEFIT.
THE ONLY THING I CAN TRUST IS MYSELF.
.....
.....
I SUPPOSE THAT'S TRUE.

I'VE ALWAYS FOUGHT ON MY POWER ALONE!!
I DON'T USE OTHERS OR CAST THEM ASIDE!!
ZAN (POINT)
BUT YOU SEE, KNIGHT OF NIGHT...
YOU'RE A WEAKLING! A COWARD! YOU CAN'T FIGHT FOR YOURSELF!!
GOOOO (WHOOSH)
YOU COULDN'T DO ANYTHING WITHOUT MANIPULATING OTHERS!
...I AM NOT LIKE YOU!
BUUN (ZMM)
WHAT ...?
HA...
WHA...
BUT YOU ARE ...
WELL, LISTEN TO THE BOY WHO ALWAYS HID BEHIND MY BACK AS HE CRIED WITH FEAR.

IF YOU WILL NOT ATTACK ME...
BUT...BUT I THOUGHT YOU WERE DEAD!
KAZU-HIRO, MY BROTH-ER...!!
...THEN I WILL HAVE TO ATTACK YOUUU !!!
RAAAAAAAH!!
GIVE ME YOUR BEST SHOT, YOSHI-YUKI.

CHAPTER 83
TERAMOTO AND THE FINAL REQUEST

BOX: CREAM MANJU YUM

PACKAGE: CREAM

PACKAGE: CHOCOLATE

ズギャーン
ZUGYAAAN (ZWOWW)
DELICIOUS !!!
MMPH!!
MY GOD!!
ぱあああああ
PAAAAA (GLOW)
SOFT, CHEWY RICE CAKE WRAPPED AROUND CREAMY CUSTARD...
IT'S THE PERFECT HARMONY OF EAST AND WEST!!
SO SMOOTH AND SOFT!
THIS IS BRILLIANT!
I... DON'T... KNOW...
WHAT WERE WE TALKING ABOUT?
.....
.....
!!!!
ガタッ
GATA (THUMP)
I'M HOME.
ガチャ
KACHA (CLICK)

AND NOW THAT YOU'RE HERE, I'D LIKE TO SPEAK WITH YOU AS WELL.
I'M HERE TO TALK WITH YOUR FATHER, SAKAKI.

TERA-MOTO-SENSEI...

NOWHERE I NEED TO TELL YOU ABOUT, AT LEAST.
NO-WHERE...
ついっ
TSUI (SPIN)

WHERE WERE YOU TODAY, URA!?

.....

SIR, SIR! CALM DOWN!
HOW CAN YOU SPEAK TO YOUR OWN FATHER THAT WAY!?
ムギッ
MUKKIII (GRRGH)

IS IT A MAN?

IT'S A MAN, ISN'T IT!?

I HAD MY SUSPICIONS, BASED ON THE WAY YOU'VE BEEN ACTING...
AS I THOUGHT ...

AND IN ORDER TO FILL THE HOLE THAT OPENED UP WITHIN YOUR SOUL, YOU BEGAN DATING A MAN.
WITHOUT A WORTHY RIVAL, YOU GREW TIRED OF KENDO AND GAVE UP THE SWORD.

THAT'S RIGHT.

WE'RE GOING TO GET SOME GIRLS TOGETHER WHO WANT ANOTHER CHANCE TO FACE OFF AGAINST YOU.
I FEEL BAD FOR HAVING DONE ALL THIS WITHOUT PERMISSION, BUT I SCHEDULED A TELEVISED KENDO MATCH ON YOUR BEHALF!!
HAAA-HA-HA-HA!
BUT REJOICE, URA!!
しゅばっ
SHUBA (ZWAP)
INDEED!
COACH TERAMOTO HAS COME TO YOUR ASSISTANCE!!

YOU MAY EVEN FIND THEM BEYOND YOUR CAPABILITIES...
GIRLS WHO HAVE BEEN HONING THEIR SKILLS FOR THE OPPORTUNITY TO TAKE YOU DOWN...

...YOU MIGHT FEEL SOMETHING WITHIN YOU CHANGE.
IF YOU COMPETE WITH THESE GIRLS...

BUT SURELY YOU WOULDN'T MIND SWINGING THE SHINAI AGAIN, JUST THIS ONE TIME?
I'M NOT ASKING FOR YOU TO RETURN TO THE TEAM.

NO!!
I HAVE NO INTENTION OF RETURNING TO KENDO!!
HOW CAN YOU SAY THAT!? AFTER ALL THAT COACH TERAMOTO HAS DONE FOR—
.....
.....
LISTEN TO ME, SAKAKI.
THE REASON I WANT YOU TO COME BACK...
...ISN'T JUST FOR YOUR SAKE.
IT'S FOR MINE AS WELL...

YOUR KENDO... IS THE VERY EMBODIMENT OF MY DREAMS.
YOUR KENDO... DISPLAYS WHAT I COULD NEVER ACHIEVE ON MY OWN.
IT HAS TO BE YOU.
NO ONE ELSE.
PLEASE, SAKAKI... IT'S MY FINAL REQUEST.
MY VERY LAST WISH.
PLEASE HELP ME...
...TO SEE THAT DREAM ONE MORE TIME!!

SO...YOU REALLY DO HATE KENDO NOW?
I'M VERY SORRY...
...BUT MY BOYFRIEND...
IT'S NOT THAT I HATE IT ANYMORE...
...I WANT TO KNOW YOUR OWN DESIRE.
SAKAKI ...
WHAT? YOU'RE NOT GOING TO DO IT BECAUSE A MAN TELLS YOU NOT TO!?
COME INTO MY ROOM.
VERY WELL.
WHAT ABOUT HOW YOU FEEL!!?

TAKIJUN

JUNYA TAKIGAWA
TAKIJUN

SIR, WHEN WAS THE LAST TIME YOU WERE IN HERE?
WHENEVER IT WAS, IT WAS TOO LONG AGO...

?
!?
.....
!!?
!?

OUR HAPPY MAGAZINE
TV-SION
8
JUNYA TAKIGAWA SPECIAL
AH!!
SFX: GOGOGOGO (RUMBLE)
I FEEL LIKE...I'VE SEEN THIS MAN BEFORE...
BOTTOM MAGAZINE: TAKIJUN
!!?
GO GO GO GO
HE...
JUNYA TAKIGAWA!!
OHH!
IT'S HIM! THE ONE ON TV...
AKA-TAKIJUN!
SFX: DODODODODO (DOOOMMM)
LOOK.
IT'S WRITTEN RIGHT HERE IN THIS ARTICLE.
TV-SION
...DESPISES CONFLICT.
HE...?
HE'S A VERY KINDHEARTED PERSON.

...WITH A GIRL WHO PURSUED SUCH A BARBARIC PASTIME AS KENDO.
SO HE WOULD NEVER FALL IN LOVE...
SFX: GOGOGOGO (RUMBLE)
MY INSTINCTS ARE SCREAMING AT ME.
DODODODO (DOOOM)
TELLING ME THAT I AM ABOUT TO WITNESS A TERROR SO GREAT THAT IT SURPASSES ALL HUMAN UNDERSTANDING!!!

BAMBOO BLADE

バンブーブレード

BAMBOO BLADE

バンブーブレード

GAKIIN (CLAANG)
GUGUGU (STRAIN)
NRRR!
HMPH!
IS THIS THE BEST YOU CAN DO, BROTHER?
BAN (LEAP)
DAN (STOMP)

DARK SLASH!!
AAAHHHH!
KA
(BOOOM)
カッ

DOKA (WHAMM)
YOUR SWORD IS INCA-PABLE OF BESTING ME!!
IN LEARNING MY IDENTITY, YOUR SWORD HAS BECOME HESITANT AND LOST!
BUT I CAN STILL KILL YOU, BROTHER, OR NOT!!
URGH...
THAT IS THE DIFFER-ENCE BETWEEN US!!

HEH!
YES, I DIED IN THAT MOMENT.
...I THOUGHT THE DEMONIC DEVIL ARMY KILLED YOU... WHEN YOU STOOD TO PROTECT ME...
BROTHER...
POWER IS EVERYTHING IN THIS WORLD!!
I DIED AND WAS BROUGHT BACK!
AND SINCE THEN I HAVE BEEN PRETENDING TO FOLLOW THEIR ORDERS, WAITING FOR MY CHANCE TO USE THIS POWER FOR MYSELF!!
BUT THE DEVIL ARMY USED MY BODY IN AN EXPERIMENT. THEY BROUGHT ME BACK TO LIFE!!
YOU ARE THE LAST OBSTACLE BETWEEN ME AND MY UTOPIA!!
BLACK DURAN, MY BROTHER.
THAT IS THE WAY THIS WORLD SHOULD BE!!!
THE POWERFUL ARE THE ONES WHO RULE!!

DIE, WEAKLING!!
GOO (BKOMM)
IS THAT...
...A TEAR...
.....?
ZAN (SHHUNK)
OR MY IMAGINATION...?
HEH.

BACK ON YOUR FEET, ARE YOU!?
THEN USE THAT SWORD!! UNLEASH YOUR FINAL ATTACK !!!
ZAKU (SHOKKI)
THE SWORD...
...ONLY LEADS TO MORE DEATH.
I CANNOT STOP YOU...
...WITH THAT THING IN MY HAND.
WHAT ...!?

I FOUGHT IN SEARCH OF MY PLACE TO DIE.
I HAD NO MEANING IN MY LIFE.
I HAD NOTHING TO PROTECT BEFORE.
IF YOU KILL ME, I WILL HAVE NO REGRETS.
PICK IT UP.
I ONLY SWUNG AROUND MY SWORD TO IMPROVE MYSELF AND NOTHING ELSE.
WHATEVER WORLD YOU WANT TO CREATE, I HAVE NO RIGHT TO STOP YOU!
YOU ARE FREE TO DO WHAT YOU WISH WITH MY LIFE.
IT'S ONLY BECAUSE OF YOU THAT I'M ALIVE RIGHT NOW.
THAT IS WHY I NO LONGER HOLD MY SWORD.
I WILL ACCEPT EVERY-THING THAT YOU ARE...
GOOO (WHOOSH)
PICK UP YOUR SWORD !!
GOOOO
ゴオオオオオ
ガオッ

I...
I...
THE SWORD ONLY BRINGS DESTRUCTION...
IT IS A SYMBOL... OF NOTHING BUT SADNESS AND HATRED.
REACH DOWN FOR THAT SWORD AND PICK IT UP, BLACK DURAN!!
...I NEVER WANTED TO SWING A SWORD...
I'M HERE FOR YOU, BROTHER.
AHHHHH!!

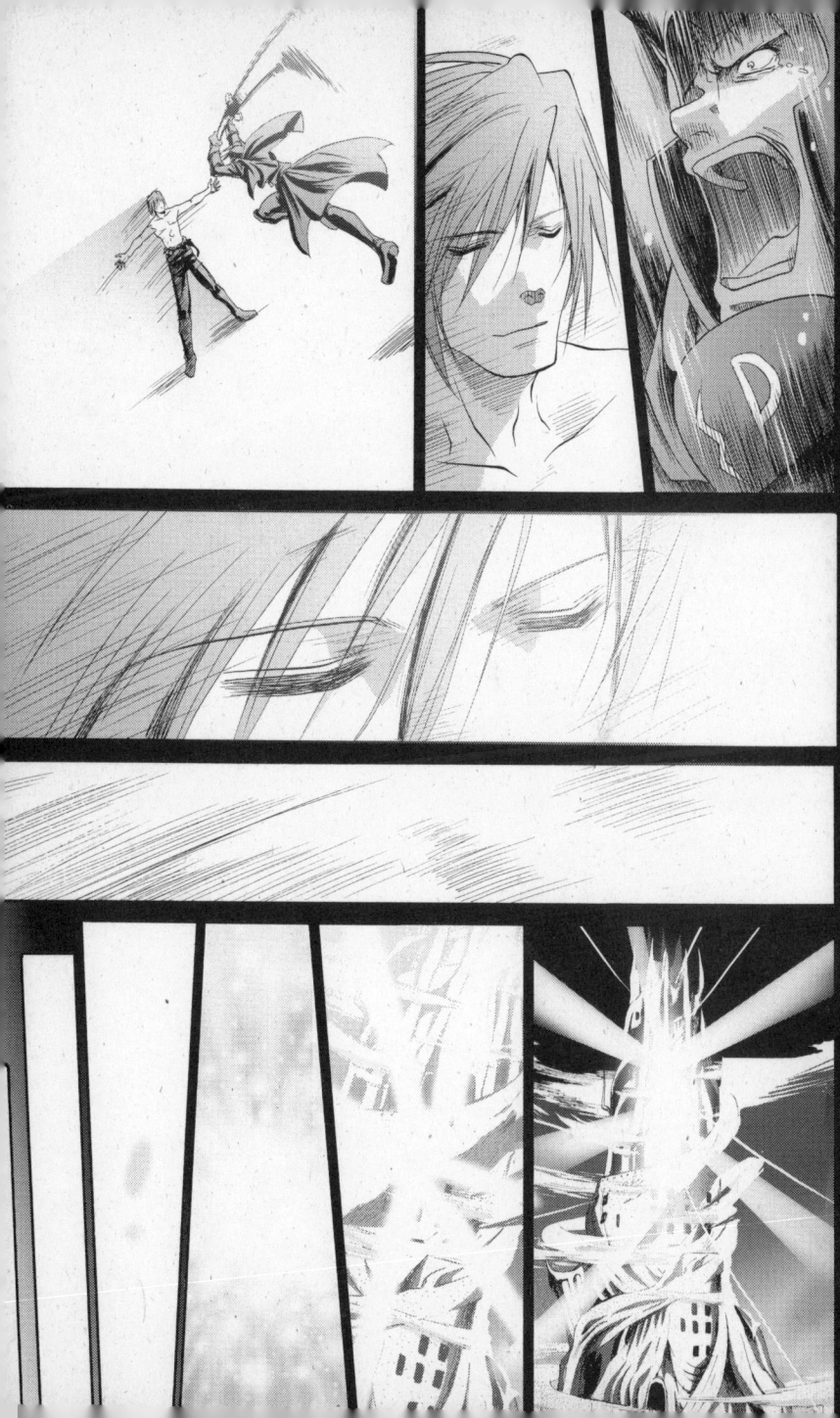

AND THAT'S WHY I HAVE GIVEN UP THE SWORD TOO.

CHAPTER 84
TERAMOTO AND URA'S ALTERNATE UNIVERSE

WE FIRST MET IN THE SPRING TWO YEARS AGO...
...IN A PARK NEAR THE SCHOOL.

MY CLASSMATES WERE IN HYSTERICS OVER THE FAMOUS ACTOR JUNYA TAKIGAWA COMING TO OUR NEIGHBOR-HOOD.
I HAD LITTLE INTEREST, AS I DIDN'T OFTEN WATCH TV.
BUT THE PARK WAS ON MY ROUTE HOME FROM SCHOOL, SO I DECIDED TO STOP BY AND SEE WHAT THE FUSS WAS ALL ABOUT.

わい わい
WAI
WAI (WHEE)

IN THAT MOMENT, I UNDERSTOOD.
...AND HE SMILED.
HE LOOKED AT ME...

HE AND I WERE CONNECTED BY AN UNBREAKABLE THREAD OF FATE...

どよっ
DOYO (MUTTER)
FURA (WOBBLE)
フラフラ
BACK! OUT OF THE FRAME!
STAY OUT OF THE SHOT!

HEY YOU!!
YOU CAN'T WALK IN THERE!!
GET OUTTA HERE!

AHH?

BUT HE IS A CELEBRITY.
I'M JUST A STUDENT.
ギャー
GYAA CAAAGH!
ガー
KAA CAAHH!
BOOO! GET HER OUT OF HERE!!
GET LOST!!
IT IS CRUEL THAT OUR HEARTS SHOULD BE SO INSEPARABLE AND YET OUR BODIES CAN NEVER BE CLOSE.
EVER SINCE THEN, I HAVE ONLY BEEN ABLE TO MEET MY LOVER THROUGH TV AND MAGAZINES.
WHOA, HANG ON A MINUTE!!
BETWEEN US...
...THERE WERE TERRIBLE, TOWERING WALLS KEEPING US APART.

YES?
S-SORRY...
CAN WE JUST TAKE A LITTLE INTER-MISSION BEFORE YOU CONTINUE?
ふう…
FUU (SIGH)

グッ GU
グッ GU (HMPH)
OKAY.
LET'S GO.
グッ GU
グッ GU
グッ GU
グッ GU
BACK INTO THAT ALTERNATE UNIVERSE!

THIS MAY SOUND LIKE A SIMPLE LINE OF DIALOGUE... BUT HE'S ACTUALLY SPEAKING TO ME.
DODODODODODO
DMMMMM
I love you.
LOOK...
HE'S EVEN SAYING IT IN THIS TV SHOW...
YOU CAN TELL IF YOU LOOK AT HIS EYES.
OH, MY POOR LOVER BOY... THIS IS THE ONLY MEANS HE HAS TO TELL ME HOW HE FEELS.

ISN'T HE SWEET?
ISN'T HE SO CARING AND DEDI-CATED?
I'VE EVEN BEEN BUSY VISITING HIS CONCERTS.
DON'T JUST IGNORE THIS !!!!
COACH TERA-MOTO!!
MY CHEST ...
GRRFH!!
!!
COACH!!
SFX: HYUKO (HURR) HYUKO
JUN-SAMAAA!
JUN-KUUN!
HE ALWAYS LOOKS AT ME AND SMILES.
KYAAA!
JUNYAAA!
キャー
KYAAA (EEEK)
EVEN IN THE HUGE CONCERT CROWDS, HE STILL FINDS A WAY TO SPOT ME IN THE MIDDLE.
キャアアアアア
KYAAAAAA

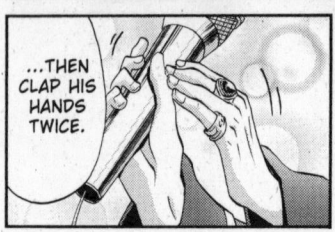

SFX: KYAAA (EEEEK) KYAAA

...I RAISED MY HAND... AGAINST MY DAUGHTER...
F-FOR THE FIRST TIME EVER...
AAHH!!
AFTER ALL, OUR HEARTS ARE ALREADY AS ONE...
...BUT I WOULD NEVER DO SUCH A MEANING-LESS THING.
ゴゴゴゴ
AFTER THE CONCERTS, THE OTHER GIRLS WOULD WAIT OUT-SIDE, HOPING TO CATCH A GLIMPSE OF HIM...
SFX: GOGOGOGOGO (RUMBLE)
SFX: GOGOGOGOGO
ゴゴゴゴゴゴゴゴゴゴゴゴゴゴ
HUFF! HUFF!
ドサッ
DOSA (THUMP)

HIS FAVORITE TYPE OF GIRL...
...IS CALM AND POLITE...
...WITH A SENSE OF KINDNESS AND CONSIDERATION FOR OTHERS.
キイ
KII (CREAK)

I AGONIZED OVER THIS.
WHAT WOULD HE THINK OF ME BEING A STUDENT OF KENDO?
シュル
SHURU (SLIP)

THAT WAS WHEN HIS NEW PROGRAM STARTED.
HE PLAYS AN ACTION HERO NAMED BLACK DURAN.
IT'S UNFORTUNATE THAT HE MUST TRANSFORM AND HIDE HIS FACE...

IF HE SAW ME SWINGING THIS IMPLEMENT, FIERCELY STRIKING OTHERS...
...WOULD HE NOT BE DISGUSTED?

IN THE END...
...HE CAST ASIDE HIS SWORD.
I COULD SEE MYSELF IN HIM, IN THE WAY HE SWINGS HIS SWORD FOR HIMSELF, NOT FOR JUSTICE.
I REALIZED HIS MESSAGE TO ME.
HE WAS TELLING ME...
...THAT I MUST PUT DOWN MY SWORD.
I DO NOT NEED IT ANY LONGER.
I RETURN THIS TO YOU.
I GAVE IN TO HIS DESIRE AND LEFT THE KENDO CLUB.
ST...
STOP, URA...

AAAH!
AAAH!
DO YOUR BEST, URA.
BIKII (CRACK)
THIS IS HOW YOU HOLD THE SHINAI, URA.
YOU'RE SO GOOD, URA! DADDY CAN'T KEEP UP ANYMORE.
LOOK, URA! I BOUGHT YOU THIS NEW SET OF BOGU FOR STARTING AT YOUR NEW SCHOOL!
AAAAAAAAAAAA!!!!!!!!!!!!
I NEED YOU, SAKAKI.
YOU'RE GOING TO BE THE BEST IN JAPAN, SAKAKI!

BAMBOO BLADE

バンブーブレード

BAMBOO BLADE
バンブーブレード

居酒屋
どぼん
WHEN A MAAAN HAS A DRIIINK~
SIGN: PUB DOBON
WE HAD UNWITTINGLY TROD INTO THE FORBIDDEN REALM OF URA SAKAKI'S TERRIFYING WORLD...
...AND WHAT HAPPENED AFTERWARD WAS HAZY AT BEST...

CHAPTER 85
THE GIRLS' SCHOOL AND THE UNIFORM THIEF

YAAAH!
PASHIN (WHACK)
PAAN (WHACK)
TOURYUU ACADEMY, KYUSHU
BANNER: GRACEFUL AS THE CRANE
YAAH!
SEY!
TEI!
雲中白鶴

スパーン
(SUPAAN (THWACK)
パーン
PAAN

SENSEI.
TERA-MOTO-SENSEI!

WHAT HAP-PENED TO SAKAKI-SAN?
HELLO?
HE WENT TO HER HOUSE TO CONVINCE HER.
スパーン
SUPAAN

SHE'S COMING BACK TO THE TEAM, ISN'T SHE!!?
IF WE HAVE SAKAKI-SAN, WE'RE UN-STOPPABLE!
ARE YOU LISTENING OR WHAT!?

SENSE!!
I JUST...

...DOOOON'T CAAAAARE...
...ANYMOOOORE...
BUILDING: OKAME TV
TOHOKU (NORTHEAST JAPAN)
...THE TV STATION WAS STILL BUSY WITH THE PLAN.
BUT PUTTING ASIDE TERAMOTO, WHO DIDN'T CARE ANYMORE...

六文女子高等学
女子
ざわざわ
ZAWA (MURMUR)
ZAWA
わいわい
WAI (WHEE)
WAI
SIGN: GIRLS'
SIGN: ROKUMON GIRLS' HIGH SCHOOL
ザワッ
ZAWA
AAAAA-HHHH !!!!

UNI-FORM THIEF !!!
WAIT UP, YOU FILTHY THIEF!!
THAT WAY!!
SFX: DODODODODO (STOMP)
WHERE!? WHERE IS HE!?!
WHAT!? NOT AGAIN!
ガタガタガタン
DAMMIT!!
SFX: GATA (THUMP) GATA GATAN
EEP!
WE'RE GONNA CUT YOUR THROAT, YOU SLIMY BASTARD!!
GET THE HELL BACK HERE!!

BA (HOP)
AHA!
EEEP!
AAAAH!
SFX: GASHA GASHAA DOGAN (CLATTERCRASH)
MOVE!
OUTTA THE WAY!!
AAAAH!
NRRRGH!!
DAAH!

ドーン
DON (BOOM)
ドカーン
DOKAAN (KABOOMM)
AAAAAHH!
WE'RE GONNA SNUFF YOU OUT, SCUM!
ROAAAH!
剣道場
SIGN: KENDO DOJO

剣道場

AHA! THE KENDO TEAM!!
WA (RAHH)
TOUKO ISHI-ZUKA-SAN!
KENDO CAPTAIN!!
ISHIZUKA-SAN, FINISH HIM!!
HERE, TOUKO!!
YOUR SHINAI!!
I'M GOOD...
IF I HAD A SHINAI IN MY HAND...
...I MIGHT ACTUALLY KILL HIM...

DO
KILL THE PIG!!
DIE, YOU PIECE OF CRAP!
WE'RE GONNA CUT YOU TO PIECES, TURD!
DO (STOMP)
THERE HE IS!
!!

GORYAAA (CRUNCH)
ガ
GA (GRAB)
KAHHK!!

NNH !!
SFX: GYURURURURURU (WHIRRRRL)
HYOEEEEEE!

GURK...

ガ
ガオオ
GAGOOO
(CRUNNNCH)
トッ
TO
(TMP)
ズン
ZUN
(THUD)

SHE WHUPPED HIS ASS!!
(WAAAA (RAHHH)
THAT WAS AWE-SOME!!
SHE'S THE BEST!!
THAT'S OUR ISHIZUKA-SAN!
SFX: GUI (YANK)
GET UP, SLOB!!
HEY! NO FALLING ASLEEP!
DON'T WORRY, SENSEI. IT'S ALREADY OVER.
WHAT SEEMS TO BE THE MATTER?
CAN YOU CALL THE POLICE?
SFX: BOKASUKA DOKA BAKI GOKYA BEKI GUSHA (CLOMP STOMP RIP CRUNCH MUNCH STOMP CRACK)
LET'S GET PRACTICE STARTED.
ARE YOU KIDDING?
ARE YOU HURT, TOUKO?
(YAAAA
DOKA (WHAM)
ORA ORA ORA !!
ORA ORA ORA !!
GO (WHAM)
BAKI (CRACK)

ER, NOT ABOUT THAT.
GA HA HA!!
TELL THEM HE FELL DOWN THE STAIRS OR WHATEVER.
YOU'RE REALLY SCARY, YOU KNOW THAT?
NO THANKS, SENSEI.
JUST A MINUTE, ISHIZUKA.
I DON'T WANT TO EXPLAIN EVERYTHING, SO CAN YOU JUST MAKE UP SOMETHING FOR THE POLICE?
CALL...?
WE JUST RECEIVED A CALL.
FROM A TV STATION.
FROM WHO?
THAT'S THE THING.

O..A
O..A
O..A
O..A
O..A
O..A!
ORA
ORA
ORAAA-
AAAAA-
AAAAA
!!!

SPECIAL STORY AZUMA AND TEST-CRAMMING HEAVEN

INDEED ...
IT'S NEARLY TIME...
GO
GO
GO
GO
GO (RUMBLE)
GO
GO
TEST SCHEDUL
MATH 1 EN
GONNN (GONGGG)

BAMBOO BLADE
バンブーブレード

BAMBOO BLADE

バンブーブレード

NURSE
保健医
せん COACH せい
師匠
HOMEROOM
担任

キ～ンコ～ン
KIINKOON (DING-DONG)
ざわ
ZAWA
ざわ
ZAWA (MURMUR)
TESTS ARE NEARLY UPON US...

SFX: GUGOGOGOGO (HRRRGH)

WE'RE ON THE DUMBER SIDE OF THINGS, SO WE NEED TO WORK HARDER THAN EVERYONE ELSE...
INDEED! WE MUST CRAM TWICE AS HARD!!
ぐゴゴゴゴ

TIME TO START STUDYING...
TSK.
CLUBS ARE OFF FROM NOW THROUGH TEST WEEK.
WE CAN DO THIS, MIYAZAKI-SAN!

WELL...
フッ。
HEH
IN MY CASE...

NORMAL
DUMB STUDENTS
NORMAL STUDENTS
GOOD STUDENTS
EASY TO UNDERSTAND!

MUROE HIGH KENDO TEAM GRADES RANKING

NYAAA (MEOW)
ニャー

SFX: DADADA (DASH)

TEKO (TEK)
てこ
TEKO
てこ

AZUMA-SAN?
TAMA-CHAAAN! DO YOU WANT TO STUDY TOGETHER?
TOTA (TUP)
トタトタ
TOTA

てこ
TEKO
てこ
TEKO
THAT'S IT!
TAMA-CHAN...

YUJI-KUN?
SHALL WE INVITE YUJI-KUN TOO?
?

I FOCUS BETTER IN A GROUP ANYWAY.
ALL RIGHT.

AND HE'S A GREAT STUDENT, SO HE WOULD BE A HUGE HELP!!
FOURTH IN THE YEAR
CAT: FIRST
I'LL BET YUJI-KUN WILL COME IF TAMA-CHAN IS WITH ME.

YEAH, OF COURSE I AM.
わいわい
WAI (WHEE)
WAI
CRAMMING FOR TESTS?

どやどや
DOYA (MURMUR)
DOYA

BYE, YOU TWO! GOOD LUCK STUDYING!
...HELPING US WITH...
MATH

GOT TO RUSH HOME AND TAKE ADVANTAGE OF NOT HAVING PRACTICE!
もじもじ…
MOJI (FIDGET)
MOJI
YUJI-KUN, WOULD YOU MIND...
UMM...
MATH
ENGLISH

SHAKA
シャカ
SHAKAAA (FIZZZ)
シャカー
...OR IS IT HIS FAULT FOR BEING SO DENSE?
IS IT OUR FAULT FOR NOT BEING CLEARER ABOUT WHAT WE NEEDED...
CUP: TEA
LEFTOVER GOOD STUDENT
ぺか〜ぺ
PEKAAA (SHINE)
...WE SHOULD VISIT THE SECOND-YEAR BUILDING.
I SUPPOSE ...
I DON'T KNOW.
WHAT NOW, TAMA-CHAN?

LET'S TAKE A LOOK.
SHUBA (LEAP)
しゅばっ
KIRINO-SENSEI, I'VE GOT IT!!

(PISHA (THUMP)
KIRINO-SENSEI, GIVE ME A BREAK...
NEXT PROB-LEM!!
NO!
HOLD IT!!
I NEED TO PEE...
WRONG!!
WHAT? BUT I THOUGHT I HAD IT RIGHT!
YOU REDUCED THE DENOMINATOR AT THE END IN THE WRONG WAY!! YOUR CALCULA-TIONS WERE COMPLETELY OFF!!

I SUPPOSE WE'RE ON OUR OWN.
WE CERTAINLY COULDN'T INTERRUPT THEM.

.....

SOME PLACE THAT IS QUIET WHERE WE CAN RELAX.
A CAFÉ, PERHAPS?
WHERE SHOULD WE STUDY?

IF YOU WANT TO CONCEN-TRATE...
...I KNOW A GOOD PLACE.
武道館
SFX: MARTIAL ARTS HALL
カラ...
KARA (RATTLE)

WHAT'S UP, YOU TWO?
WE DON'T HAVE PRACTICE TODAY.
TESTS, REMEMBER?
HUH?
WE WENT TO THE FACULTY ROOM TO BORROW THE KEY...
...BUT IT WAS ALREADY OUT. I GUESS YOU MUST HAVE TAKEN IT.
WE KNOW. WE'RE HERE TO STUDY.
IN THE DOJO?
STUDY?
ACTUALLY, I FORGOT WE WERE OFF FOR TESTS AT FIRST.
BUT SINCE I'M HERE ALREADY, MIGHT AS WELL GET SOME CLEANING DONE.
NOW I'M RE-ARRANGING AWARDS.
パタ
PATA
パタ
PATA (FLAP)

SIGN: SOUL IN EVERY PITCH

I FEEL LIKE YOU KIDS ARE DANGEROUSLY CLOSE TO FORGETTING THAT I'M ACTUALLY A BONA FIDE TEACHER!
THIS IS PER-FECT!
I NEED TO PROVE I COMMAND YOUR RESPECT!
DOOH!
SFX: DOON (BOOM)
HA-HA-HA!
OKAY! IN FACT, WHY DON'T I HELP YOU OUT WITH YOUR STUDIES?
WHAT? SENSEI!?
SFX: GOSO (RUSTLE) GOSO
PARA (FLIP)
LET'S SEE...
BOOK: ENGLISH, EENGURISHU
WELL, WE WERE GOING TO FOCUS ON ENGLISH TODAY...
WHAT SUBJECT ARE WE STARTING WITH?
BOOK: ENGLISH

いんぐりっしゅ

BOOK: EENGURISHU

DAMN IT AAAAAAALLLL!!
SENSEI!!!
.....
.....
I GUESS WE'RE STUDYING...
...BY OURSELVES...
HUH? IT'S OPEN.
IS SOMEONE HERE?

SFX: BUUU (BOOO)

OYO?
EVERYONE'S HERE.
HOW ABOUT THAT?
I GUESS EVERYONE SHOWED UP IN THE END.
OOOH!
IT JUST GOES TO SHOW...
...THAT WE ALL LOVE IT IN HERE.
AND THE FACT THAT I BELONG HERE TOO...
...MAKES ME SO HAPPY.
I'M GLAD I JOINED...
...THE MUROE HIGH KENDO CLUB.

KARI
KARI
KARI

TRANSLATION NOTES

Common Honorifics

No honorific: Indicates familiarity or closeness; if used without permission or reason, addressing someone in this manner would constitute an insult.

***-san*:** The Japanese equivalent of Mr./Mrs./Miss. If a situation calls for politeness, this is the fail-safe honorific.

***-sama*:** Conveys great respect; may also indicate that the social status of the speaker is lower than that of the addressee.

***-kun*:** Used most often when referring to boys, this indicates affection or familiarity. Occasionally used by older men among their peers, but it may also be used by anyone referring to a person of lower standing.

***-chan*:** An affectionate honorific indicating familiarity used mostly in reference to girls; also used in reference to cute persons or animals of either gender.

***-senpai*:** Used as a suffix or alone to address one's upperclassmen.

***kouhai*:** The opposite of *senpai*, used to address younger schoolmates or team members.

***-sensei*:** A respectful term for teachers, artists, or high-level professionals.

Page 23

Bromide: A high-quality, usually promotional photograph of a celebrity. The name is based on the term "bromide paper," a type of photograph paper that contains the chemical bromide. These glossy photos were first advertised in Japan using the term bromide, and the name stuck, even when actual bromide paper isn't used.

Page 29

Shamoji: A large, flat paddle used specifically for stirring and serving rice.

Page 38

Hoichi the Earless: A figure from Japanese mythology, Hoichi the Earless was a blind minstrel haunted by ghosts that tricked him into thinking he was performing music for a feudal lord every night. When a priest discovered the treachery, he painted the kanji for a protective sutra all over Hoichi's body, only forgetting to cover his ears. When Hoichi was next visited by the ghosts and the sutra protected his body, they ripped off his exposed ears in rage.

Page 43

***Ochugen*:** A gift-giving occasion centered around July 15th. Gifts are delivered to people to whom the giver owes a formal or personal debt, such as a physician, a teacher, a helpful relative, etc. Perhaps *Ochugen Cop* is a hard-boiled detective who never forgets to display his appreciation.

Page 53

Gyokuryuuki: A famous, real-life high school kendo meet that is held annually in the city of Fukuoka in Kyushu. The Shouryuuki meet depicted in Volume 1 of *Bamboo Blade* was originally an homage to this tournament.

Page 115

***Manju*:** A traditional confection consisting of a rounded, steamed bun made of flour and rice powder with a sweet filling inside, typically a sweet red bean paste (*anko*).

Page 126

Takijun: In Japanese, nicknames given to people, bands, TV shows, games, anime, and so on are often abbreviated in a way that takes the first syllable or two of each word into a short and catchy phrase. The "Takijun" shown here is easy to understand when you see the name Junya Takigawa placed in its original Japanese order of family name first and given name last: **Taki**-gawa **Jun**-ya. (The show *Burnish Academy* is the same deal: it's an abbreviation of the fictional comedy duo that hosts it, **Burni**-ng Da-**sh**.)

BAMBOO BLADE
バンブーブレード
POLITICS AND ECONOMICS

OMAKE MANGA THEATER ④

TERAMOTO-SENSEI AND THE BAD STUDENTS

SFX: KYUPON (POP)

OMAKE MANGA THEATER ❸

FATHER AND DAUGHTER'S COOKING

OMAKE MANGA THEATER ❷

SATORI AND THE UNREMOVABLE MEMO

ARM: BURNISH ACADEMY VIDEO

SFX: PIIPOO (WEE-OO) PIIPOO

OMAKE MANGA THEATER ❶

SAYAKO AND THE RETURN OF THE FAMILY MEETING

AFTERWORD

THE BAMBOO BLADE THAT YOU SEE IN THESE PAGES IS A COLLABORATION BETWEEN IGARASHI-SENSEI AND I, SO IT ISN'T CREATED WITH COMPLETE AND TOTAL ABANDON. IN THE SERIES WHERE I HANDLE BOTH STORY AND ART, I'M FREE TO DO WHATEVER I FEEL LIKE, BUT *BAMBOO BLADE* AND MY OTHER CURRENT SERIES, *MATERIAL PUZZLE ZERO KREUZ*, ARE DRAWN BY OTHER ARTISTS, SO I DON'T PUT QUITE AS MUCH POISONOUS CYNICISM INTO THEM. I DO MY BEST NOT TO LOAD THEM WITH SNEAKY, UNPREDICTABLE PLOT TWISTS AND SURREAL GAGS. THE GOAL IS NOT QUITE AS MUCH ABOUT SATISFYING MYSELF AS SATISFYING THE READERS' DESIRES.

THE WORLD AROUND US IS CURRENTLY IN THE WILDLY POPULAR PART OF THE BOOM-AND-BUST CYCLE WITH REGARDS TO OLD MEN, SO IT'S REALLY ONLY NATURAL THAT CHARACTERS LIKE COACH TERAMOTO AND URA'S PAPA BECOME THE FOCUS OF THE STORY, BUT FOR SOME REASON, MY EDITOR STARTED SULKING.

"I HATE THIS. I'VE HAD ENOUGH OF THE OLD MEN. I WANNA SEE GIRLS. DRAW MORE GIRLS."

THIS EDITOR IS A HUGE FAN OF MY MANGA, SO HE TRIES TO SEE WHERE I'M TAKING THE STORY BEFORE ANYONE ELSE. AS I'M DRAWING THE CHAPTER, HE GOES,

"IS IT READY? IS IT READY?"

AND THEN HE STARTS BEGGING FOR DETAILS.

"WHAT'S GOING TO HAPPEN NEXT WITH THIS?"

BUT FINDING OUT AHEAD OF TIME RUINS ALL THE SUSPENSE AND EXCITEMENT, SO WHEN I TELL HIM TO BE PATIENT AND READ IT IN THE MAGAZINE, HE SNAPS AND SCREAMS,

"NO WAY, MAN!"

WHAT'S HIS PROBLEM ANYWAY?

COACH TERAMOTO

I'M TRYING TO FULFILL THE READERS' NEEDS BY PUMPING OUT LOTS OF OLD MEN, BUT SINCE IT IS THANKS TO THIS EDITOR THAT I HAVE A SERIES AT ALL, I FEEL OBLIGED TO SATISFY HIM. IT'S REALLY HARD TO CREATE A GREAT MANGA WHEN YOU'RE STUCK BETWEEN A ROCK AND A HARD PLACE LIKE THIS. I'M WRITING THIS MESSAGE HERE IN THE HOPES THAT YOU ALL UNDERSTAND MY PLIGHT. PLEASE KEEP IT IN MIND AS THE REST OF THE STORY UNFOLDS.

MASAHIRO TOTSUKA

BACKSTAGE AFTERWORD ♥

STAFF

STORY-
TOTSUKA-SENSEI
ART-
AGURI
EDITOR-
THE ERO-RIST
MAC ASSISTANT-
INA-SAN
BACKGROUNDS-
OREO-SAN, MAEDA-SAN
SCANNER-
DAD
SHOULDER MASSAGES-
LITTLE BRO

Can't wait for the next volume? You don't have to!

Keep up with the latest chapters of some of your favorite manga every month online in the pages of YEN PLUS!

Visit us at
www.yenplus.com
for details!

Maximum Ride © James Patterson, Illustrations © Hachette Book Group • Gossip Girl © Alloy Entertainment, Illustrations © Hachette Book Group • Daniel X © James Patterson, Illustrations © Hachette Book Group • Soulless © 2009 by Tofa Borregaard / Illustrations © Hachette Book Group, Inc. • K-ON! © Kakifly / HOUBUNSHA

WANT TO READ *MANGA* ON YOUR IPAD?

Now for iPhone too!

Download the *YEN PRESS* app for full volumes of some of our bestselling titles!

Nightschool © Svetlana Chmakova

BAMBOO BLADE ⑩

MASAHIRO TOTSUKA
AGURI IGARASHI

Translation: Stephen Paul

Lettering: Terri Delgado

BAMBOO BLADE Vol. 10 © 2009 Masahiro Totsuka, Aguri Igarashi / SQUARE ENIX CO., LTD. All rights reserved. First published in Japan in 2009 by SQUARE ENIX CO., LTD. English translation rights arranged with SQUARE ENIX CO., LTD. and Hachette Book Group through Tuttle-Mori Agency, Inc.

Translation © 2011 by SQUARE ENIX CO., LTD.

All rights reserved. Except as permitted under the U.S. Copyright Act of 1976, no part of this publication may be reproduced, distributed, or transmitted in any form or by any means, or stored in a database or retrieval system, without the prior written permission of the publisher.

The characters and events in this book are fictitious. Any similarity to real persons, living or dead, is coincidental and not intended by the author.

Yen Press
Hachette Book Group
237 Park Avenue, New York, NY 10017

www.HachetteBookGroup.com
www.YenPress.com

Yen Press is an imprint of Hachette Book Group, Inc. The Yen Press name and logo are trademarks of Hachette Book Group, Inc.

First Yen Press Edition: September 2011

ISBN: 978-0-316-18936-1

10 9 8 7 6 5 4 3 2 1

BVG

Printed in the United States of America